Creepy

Ladybirds

Siân Smith

Raintree

www.raintreepublishers.co.uk
Visit our website to find out more information about Raintree books.

To order:
☎ Phone 0845 6044371
🖷 Fax +44 (0) 1865 312263
🖳 Email myorders@raintreepublishers.co.uk

Customers from outside the UK please telephone +44 1865 312262

Raintree is an imprint of Capstone Global Library Limited, a company incorporated in England and Wales having its registered office at 7 Pilgrim Street, London, EC4V 6LB – Registered company number: 6695582

Text © Capstone Global Library Limited 2013
First published in hardback in 2013
Paperback edition first published in 2014
The moral rights of the proprietor have been asserted.

Edited by Dan Nunn, Rebecca Rissman, and Sian Smith
Designed by Joanna Hinton-Malivoire
Picture research by Ruth Blair
Originated by Capstone Global Library Ltd
Production by Victoria Fitzgerald
Printed and bound in China

ISBN 978 1 406 24139 6 (hardback)
16 15 14 13 12
10 9 8 7 6 5 4 3 2 1

ISBN 978 1 406 24153 2 (paperback)
17 16 15 14 13
10 9 8 7 6 5 4 3 2 1

British Library Cataloguing in Publication Data
Smith, Sian.
   Ladybirds. – (Creepy crawlies)
   1. Ladybugs–Pictorial works–Juvenile literature.
   I. Title II. Series
   595.7′69-dc22

Acknowledgements
We would like to thank the following for permission to reproduce photographs: Dreamstime.com pp.9 (© Abubjsm), 22 (© Kodo34), 23 (© Aetmeister); iStockphoto pp.6 (© Judy Barranco), 13 (© Paul Grecaud); Photoshot p.15 (© Juniors Tierbildarchiv); Shutterstock pp.4 (©Tischenko Irina), 4 (© Matej Ziak), 5 (© irin-k), 5 (© Yummyphotos), 7 (© irin-k), 8 (© Tito Wong), 8 (© Alta Oosthuizen), 9 (© Henrik Larsson), 9 (© Kletr), 10 (© Yellowj), 10 (© Chepko Danil Vitalevich), 10, 10 (© irin-k), 11 (© Yellowj), 12 (© Christian Mueller), 14 (© Sean Gladwell), 14 (© nimblewit), 16 (© Kletr), 17 (© Pavel Mikoska), 18 (© D. Kucharski & K. Kucharska), 19 (© Christine vanReeuwyk), 20 (© Smit), 21 (© Sebastian Knight), 22 (© Leigh Prather), 22 (© irin-k), 22 (© kurt_G), 22 (© Vital Che), 23 (© Alex Staroseltsev), 23 (© photolinc).

Front cover photograph reproduced with permission of Shutterstock (© irin-k).

The publisher would like to thank Michael Bright for his help in the preparation of this book.

Every effort has been made to contact copyright holders of any material reproduced in this book. Any omissions will be rectified in subsequent printings if notice is given to the publisher.

Contents

Spots in the garden

What is this creepy crawly?
In the garden there are lots.

They look very small and shiny,
and are covered in tiny spots.

If you said it was a bird,
you won't get any blame.

But it's actually a beetle,
and ladybird is its name.

What colour is a ladybird?
Most are black and red.

Some are yellow with black spots, or brown with white spots instead.

Counting the spots on a ladybird, won't let you know its age.

Ladybirds can have different numbers of spots. That's just the way they are made.

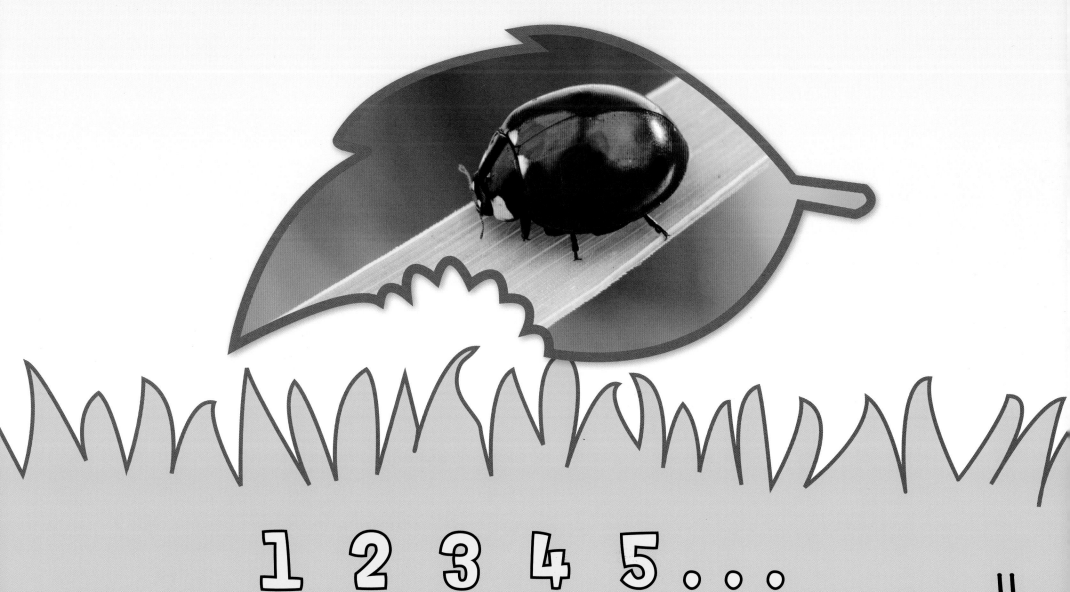

1 2 3 4 5...

Shell secrets

Ladybirds have a secret.
They keep it under their shell.

Hidden there are two big wings,
which help them to fly really well.

wing

To stay safe from birds and spiders, a ladybird can hide its head.

They can also roll over onto their backs, and pretend that they are dead.

Ladybird lunches

Ladybirds eat greenfly and aphids, and consider them a treat.

aphid

Some types of ladybird do eat plants, but most eat only meat.

Yum

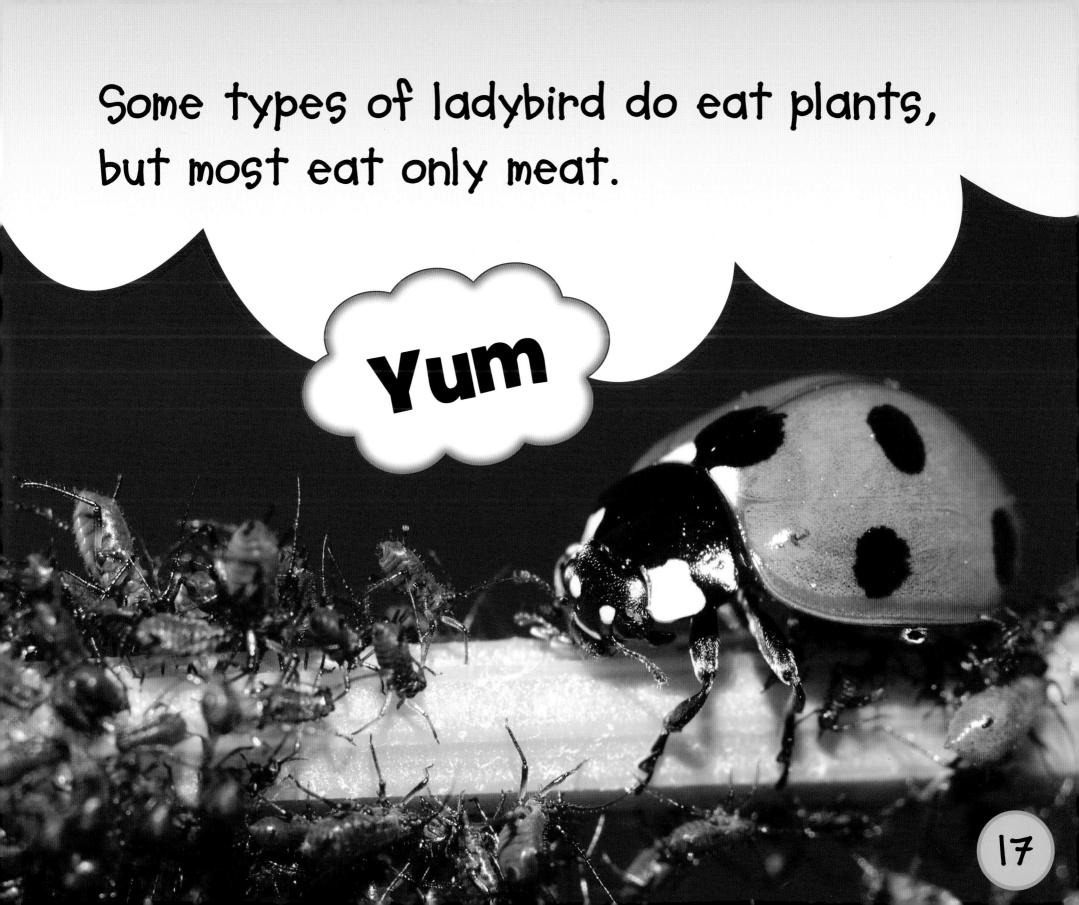

Strange babies

Compared to their mum and dad, ladybird babies can look strange.

They start out as small black larvae, and then they start to change.

Out in the cold

Ladybirds get together in winter, both young ladybirds and old.

They find a place where they can all go to sleep, when the weather starts to get cold.

21

Looking for ladybirds

Can you find two ladybirds here?
There's an adult and a child.

They are hiding somewhere near these plants, just like they do in the wild.

Did you know?

A group of ladybirds is called a loveliness of ladybirds.

Index

24